MY FIRST LOOK AT HOLIDAYS

VALENTINE'S DAY IS A WINTER HOLIDAY

Valentine's Day

VALERIE BODDEN

CREATIVE EDUCATION

Published by Creative Education

123 South Broad Street, Mankato, Minnesota 56001

Creative Education is an imprint of The Creative Company

Designed by Rita Marshall

Photographs by Archive Photos, Bruce Carr, Getty Images (Ken Tannenbaum), Keystone

Press, Paul McMahon, Richard Nowitz, Bonnie Sue Rauch

Cover illustration © 1996 Roberto Innocenti

Printed in the United States of America

Library of Congress Cataloging-in-Publication Data

Bodden, Valerie. Valentine's Day / by Valerie Bodden.

p. cm. — (My first look at holidays)

Includes bibliographical references.

ISBN 1-58341-371-5

I. Valentine's Day—Juvenile literature. I. Title. II. Series.

GT4925.B64 2004   394.2618—dc22   2004056160

First edition 9 8 7 6 5 4 3 2 1

Valentine's Day

A Man Named Valentine

Valentine's Day is a day for friendship and love. People celebrate Valentine's Day on February 14.

Many people believe that Valentine's Day is named after a **priest**. His name was Valentine. Long ago, a law said that people could not get married. Valentine thought this law was wrong. So he married people in secret.

A PICTURE OF SAINT VALENTINE (WITH LONG BEARD)

Because he broke the law, Valentine was put in jail. There, he fell in love with the jailer's daughter. The girl was blind, but Valentine did a **miracle** to make her see again.

Valentine was killed. But before he died, he sent the girl a note. He signed it, "From Your Valentine." Valentine died on February 14. Years later, he became a **saint**.

Long ago, people did not
give Valentine cards.
Instead, they said or
sang their Valentine message.

MANY VALENTINE CARDS SHOW FLOWERS OR HEARTS

Valentine's Day Decorations

The colors for Valentine's Day are red, pink, and white. Hearts are the most popular decorations for Valentine's Day. Hearts mean "love." So do roses.

Pictures of Cupid are popular decorations, too. Cupid is a baby with wings. He carries a bow and arrows. One story says that he shoots his arrows at people. If an arrow hits someone, he or she will fall in love.

More cards are sent for

Valentine's Day than

for any other special day

except Christmas.

Many Valentine's Day decorations have ribbons and lace on them. Some have "XOXO" on them. The letter "X" is a kiss, and the letter "O" is a hug.

VALENTINE CARDS

Today, many people send special cards called Valentines. They send Valentines to friends and family. The cards have pictures or messages that can be sweet or funny.

"Valentine" has come to mean "love"

Many Valentines have pictures of hearts and flowers. Some have pictures of Cupid. Many cards say, "Be my Valentine" or "Be mine."

People have been sending Valentines for hundreds of years. Long ago, people made their own Valentines. The cards were usually big and fancy.

Te amo means "I love you"

in Spanish.

Ich liebe dich means

"I love you" in German.

THIS VALENTINE IS ALMOST 100 YEARS OLD

Today, some people still make their own Valentines. Other people buy Valentines from stores that sell cards. Some even send e-mail Valentines!

CANDY, FLOWERS, AND CHOCOLATE

Many schools have Valentine's Day parties. Kids give cards to their friends and **classmates**. Sometimes they give candy or other treats, too.

Valentine chocolates come in many shapes and flavors

Many people give flowers on Valentine's Day. Red roses are the most popular. Some people give chocolate. Valentine's Day chocolate usually comes in a heart-shaped box. Other people give jewelry or teddy bears for Valentine's Day.

On Valentine's Day, show your friends and family how special they are. Make them a card. Give them a present. Say, "I love you!"

Americans buy more
than 110 million roses for
Valentine's Day every year.

A RED ROSE MEANS "I LOVE YOU"

Hands-on: Valentine Cookies

These sweet treats are fun to eat!

What You Need

Vanilla wafer cookies

Chocolate "kisses," unwrapped

Valentine candy hearts

Cookie sheet

Oven

What You Do

1. Put the vanilla wafer cookies on the cookie sheet.
2. Set a chocolate "kiss" in the middle of each cookie.
3. Have a grown-up bake the cookies at 200 °F (90 °C) for five minutes.
4. When the cookies come out of the oven, carefully press a candy heart into the chocolate on each.
5. Let the cookies cool. Then, enjoy your Valentine's Day treats!

CUPID MAKES PEOPLE FALL IN LOVE

Index

Words to Know

classmates—kids who are in the same class at school

miracle—when something happens that seems impossible

priest—a person who teaches people about God

saint—a person who lived a good life and did miracles before he or she died

Read More

Haugen, Brenda. *Valentine's Day*. Minneapolis, Minn.: Picture Window Books, 2004.

Klingel, Cynthia, and Robert B. Noyed. *Valentine's Day*. Chanhassen, Minn.: The Child's World, 2003.

Rosinsky, Natalie M. *Valentine's Day*. Minneapolis, Minn.: Compass Point Books, 2003.

Explore the Web

Billy Bear's Happy Valentine's Day

http://www.billybear4kids.com/holidays/valentin/fun.htm

Kids Domain: Valentine's Day http://www.kidsdomain.com/holiday/val

Kids' Turn Central: Valentine's Day

http://www.kidsturncentral.com/holidays/valentines.htm